VIV   MATVEEVA

WHILE
YOU'RE
WAITING

*A Love Letter for
Expectant Adoptive Parents*

While You're Waiting...
A Love Letter For Expectant Adoptive Parents

Difference Press, Washington, D.C., USA
© Viv Matveeva, 2021

ISBN: 978-1-68309-280-3

Cover Design: Nakita Duncan
Editing: Cory Hott

This book is lovingly dedicated to my teachers:

Daria and Alex, for setting the bar on resilience and not running away at the airport. Cole, for joining me in being "something bigger and better than ourselves." Dad, for showing me how to love unconditionally. Mom, for giving me sweetness.

Grown up daughters are women writers unfolding their own life-giving story of the love between parent and child.

TABLE OF CONTENTS

CHAPTER 1

A LOVE LETTER TO EXPECTANT PARENTS EVERYWHERE

Dear Cousin Dove,

I received your email today about signing the adoption papers, you did it! I could hear the excitement in your voice, picturing your curly chestnut locks swirling in the air as you stood from the adoption agent's desk and bear hugged your partner. The two of you have so much love and wisdom to offer a child; you might be the coolest couple I know with your relentless commitment to busting through glass ceilings, while being the most devoted volunteer in his advocacy campaign.

I remember when you used to visit us each summer. We would camp out in my room for hours at a time as that was far better than sizzling in the desert heat outside. While our mom's laughed about weird things, and whispered about their lives, you would take every animal and gadget in my room to construct a bustling village of families lounging, cooking, building, and dancing on my bedroom floor.

I wish I could guarantee that is what having a family will look like. I suppose I can agree that the range of colorful activity you set up in your imaginary land can exist with adopting a child, but it may not be exactly what you think. I've often recognized myself in your altruistic beliefs, but I now know there is more to our instinctual and salacious need to design these mini-villages of affection, adoration, care and fun when we were children. We want to love, and be loved.

In your email, you asked me about our adoption experience and for some advice. The very best piece I can offer you right now is to take stock of your own emotional and physical health, your relationship, and address any areas that need attention before you bring your child home.

An adoptive child inherently carries hurt from the separation related to their birth parent, and depending on the circumstances, has a range of high-needs from their new family. They will desperately need you to have your act together. They won't care so much about the color of the paint on the wall in their bedroom, or which bedding you choose. They need you to know how to practice enduring patience, compassionate understanding, tender care, relentless, love and determination. While you're waiting with arms open wide, become masterful in providing this to yourself in order to consistently give it to your soon to be precious adopted child.

Big Love,
Me

CHAPTER 2

WAITING, STUCK IN WAITING, STILL WAITING

It was almost midnight in mid-January in Russia, a bitter brutal blah blue cold. Sergei had escorted us safely from our hotel, and Natalia translated our passage from ticket counter to waiting area. Sergei was like Owl Eyes in *The Great Gatsby*, holding constant awareness of our journey, and striking a balance in protecting us from the bureaucracy of the country he served. Waiting for the train, that would deliver the kids and myself overnight to arrive in Moscow the next morning, was the ravine... between my former life and the one ahead. The one in which I became caretaker, security guard, cheerleader, CEO, secretary, cook, taxi-driver, nurse, housekeeper, protector, mediator, and mom.

We stood together in our little silent cluster as travelers passed hurriedly by us. I don't believe I saw any of them smile, but neither were we. The kids were white as ghosts, and were as motionless as our luggage sitting at our feet. Sergei and Natalia waited with us almost like a father and mother would in the old movies where their child was boarding a train for combat. They had taken care of the logistics of our life during our time in St. Petersburg, yet they were helpless in the realm of soothing the kids during this strange and massive disruption to their lives in the orphanage. I could see Sergei and Natalia's concern for me in their eyes. They had the wisdom of life in Russia, and knew then, long before I did, the mountains to traverse ahead of us. It was a bittersweet moment together before I embarked the 8-hour train ride alone, never to see them again, with my two foreign speaking toddlers I'd known for only 10-days.

STUCK IN WAITING

When waiting for a train or plane, you might read, check on the schedule awaiting you at the other end of your trip, call, text, tap, scroll your phone stuck in a moment between then and next. How wonderful it can be to find yourself "stuck in a moment" of awe, love at first sight. Other familiar situations of stuckness include fastened to a seat on an airplane as it sits delayed on a runway, stuck in traffic, or stuck at work waiting for a server to fire back up. These all suggest a cease in motion out of your control. Other times, you might find yourself in a sticky situation, stuck in the mud, or *Stuck Inside Of Mobile With The Memphis Blues Again* (thank you Bob Dylan). There's also the quagmire of being stuck in indecision. The latter is typically serving you in some way you called forth without even knowing it! It could be akin to procrastinating on a project, lack of desire for your partner, or fear of rejection when you apply for that dream job.

How often do you explore the currents of electricity in static moments? A lack of awareness or presence in the body is often shared by the states of stuck and waiting. By the way, this is different than getting lost in a foreign city due to not planning ahead. I'm referring to how we numb ourselves, superficially fill the void, or get mired in anxiety while waiting. There are hidden gems in what you might uncover when you take notice of what's happening in the in-between... while waiting.

There is a gracefulness, something understated, a richness in simplicity when you shift the framework of waiting due to circumstance. For, the place of perceived immobility can be utterly compelling. I can promise you that you won't get all the things done that you wanted to do before having children. Use the time to reclaim or recharge your health, become a master at patience, learn how to get grounded, and put yourself together when life breaks you open.

I promise it is entirely worth it, and your life will be enriched through adoption in unimaginable quantities. I know the waiting can be maddening, and the thoughts of your adoption are equally frightening and exciting. I imagine you have many questions about the process and are researching all angles of it. You've likely searched the internet in hopes of a glimpse into where your child may come from, and what he or she looks like. You may be in an endless loop of searching for that one sweet facial expression across the screen that will affirm your dream of becoming an adoptive parent.

STILL WAITING

By this point, you have answered the pull within your heart about adoption. Theodore Roosevelt said, "in a moment of decision, the best thing you can do is the right thing to do. The worst thing you can do is nothing." Your future adoptive child is so very fortunate you've begun the process that will result in them finally having a chance to be loved and cared for by their parent(s).

There is purity in the desire to extend yourself to another, especially a child who will be completely dependent on you. You know you have so much love to give, yet, are completely petrified by the unknown, not to mention your secret fear about whether or not you are really ready. Please let me confirm that feeling a belly-aching mix of exhilaration and terror is common. Imagining the sweet hugs, throwing the ball with them, and nurturing their growth brings warm feelings. There are other feelings you may or may not have, and thoughts you may or may not have said out loud. What if the child is ill? What if they don't look like me? What if they don't like me?

I'm curious how often I've heard people use the term "baby of my own" during my adoption experience.

Some might say, "I think adoption is wonderful, but I want a baby of my own," or "Could you not have a baby of your own?" These themes suggest an unhealthy - proprietary relationship between a parent and a child, which can occur in any family. If left unchecked, it has the potential for contributing to negative development or behavior in the child.

An adoptive child is as much a child of you and the family as a biological child is when you think of it in terms of sweat equity, as in how much are you truly willing to unconditionally regard, accept, and love the child. There certainly is a list of important differences in the dynamics that come with children of different backgrounds, particularly where trauma or neglect occurred. However, for many parents, their mindset has the potential to positively or negatively influence their child's experience.

Equipping yourself with the wholehearted commitment in becoming an adoptive parent begs for self-agency, self-care, self-love, and the raw truth within oneself. A way in begins with a keen skill in self-awareness, discovered through reflection and contemplation. Slowing down to notice what is happening in your inner world happens through listening, really, really listening.

I wish I could tell you not to be scared. I can't do that, but what I can offer is a glimpse into our experience, as well as the experience of some of the people I have worked with in my therapeutic practice. You wouldn't be reading this book if you weren't a potentially great fit for adoption. It's an indicator that you are careful, considerate and compassionate. These are certainly necessary characteristics of an adoptive parent. Gaining clarity on where you are in your life in terms of satisfaction, thriving, healing the past, and reaching aspirations will pay dividends in the next steps of adoption.

As I describe more of our imperfectly perfect story, I will encourage you to fine-tune your emotional intelligence, unfold your whole story, and develop a contemplative practice about the adoption and parenting decision. You will develop a new skill in noticing the gift of the messages awaiting deep within your center.

The process of bringing the pieces of you together will inform your parenting style, and relationship with your child. I know there are important reasons why you considered adoption in the first place, and you may or may not want to face or admit your concerns or fears.

"It was the kind of whole certainty, however independent of the sum of its facts, that can make walking backwards more than normally hazardous, and I bumped smack into a baby carriage."
– J.D. Salinger, Nine Stories

This book is about you, and truly connecting the pull toward adoption by considering where you are now, and where you come from related to the dream of adoption. We will do this through self-reflection and I'll guide you by asking you important questions, such as how your relationship with your family of origin influenced you through childhood and this decision. These relationships, as well as other elements of your life, establish patterns for how you relate to others, in particular how you may parent a child.

YOU'VE DECIDED, NOW WHAT?

Adoption is bold, compassionate, and kind. Beginning the process and adopting a child is one of the most, if not the absolute most, challenging and important things you will do in your life. In order to get to that point of beginning, there is much to consider, such as where to adopt, when to adopt, finances, timing, what agency to use, boy or girl, infant, toddler or older child, foster, private, domestic or international. This process requires knowledge, knowing how to get resourced, attuned discernment, patience, self-efficacy, and a sense of clarity and resolve in your heart. The adoptive child experiences trauma earlier than most, in the form of a breech of trust in their relationship with their biological parents. The adoptive child needs needs you to be ready to make them feel safe and protected.

The focus of this book is you – meeting you on the bridge between the decision to adopt a child, and finally bringing him or her home. But first, let's more fully consider what this book is not - as a way to clear the path ahead of us. There are individuals and organizations who specialize and work in these fields. You'll find helpful books written by adoptive parents encompassing one or more aspects of their post-decision to adopt. There are many clinical books, videos and workshops available on the adoption process, from general to specific topics. This book is not a conclusive and all-promising guarantee that you can achieve a blissful and successful adoption experience. Much of that is relative to how you step into the process yourself, and the degree to which you can experience love and fulfillment without guarantees. You will take a deep dive into your inner world by considering the questions in the following chapters, beginning with peeling back the curtain on what's behind your pull toward adoption.

SELF REFLECTION AND CONTEMPLATION

Self-awareness will be harnessed in this book. You will be challenged to notice your inner world in a deeply soft way, and become an expert listener of your heart and mind. One of the greatest gifts we can offer the people we care about, as well as ourselves, is authenticity. The absence of this precipitates inevitable disruption, sometimes destruction, in relationship with self and others. A contemplative practice is where we begin by oxygenating self-awareness, and learning to get comfortable with inaction, the white space, waiting, and keeping quiet...

> *If we were not so single minded about keeping*
> *our lives moving, and for once could do nothing, per-*
> *haps a huge silence might interrupt this sadness of never*
> *understanding ourselves...*
> **– Pablo Neruda**

In the context of becoming parent, the children deserve a chance where they are not the objects of a parent's subconscious void. Building the muscles around practicing self-reflection is not particularly easy in the beginning. It's akin to a common meditation practice where there are always other things to do; distractions seem to be more welcome and urgent, and solid intentions often do not translate into action. However, the result of finding ample stillness to get curious, and then listen without judgement, has the power of a more rich relationship with yourself, and therefore others.

WHILE YOU' WAITING...

Begin to consider the term and act of "listening." What simply comes to mind? What does the word *listen* feel like, and mean to you? What experience(s) have you had that stand out around listening and being heard?

Answer, on a scale of 1 to 5, (strongly disagree to strongly agree):

- I'm comfortable spending time alone.
- I'm comfortable in silence.
- I can stand back from situations and consider what went well, and/or not so well.
- I can consider what I may do differently the next time, without beating myself up.
- I am already enough.
- I am totally loveable.
- I take extremely good care of my physical, emotional, and spiritual health.

Consider how tending to the need of a child is inherent in parenting. Carrying neediness into parenting drains energy. One definition of love is it's the extension of oneself to another. How can one effectively extend oneself, in the name of love, without wholehearted self-love? Simply put, how can we love another if we don't know how to love ourselves?

This book meets you on the rollercoaster of "waiting." Passivity inside of waiting is an option. Listening when life demands our attention, commands grit, and compels compassion offers the potential for a wildly enriching ride. Please note that all names and other identifying details have been changed in respect and protection of the individual's experience and identity.

CHAPTER 3

WHAT DOES IT MEAN TO BE A REAL MOM

I am a mom to two resilient, wise, beautiful and funny teenagers: Daria and Alex, adopted from Tikhvin, Russia twelve-years ago. A tradition in Russia is to refer to children by their nickname, which has endearing variations. My son's Russian-given name is Alexander. The orphanage caregivers would refer to him as Sasha, Sashka, Sonka, and Sashki. It was an example of the adoration and affection the children received at the orphanage. I witnessed this firsthand on the day I was to pick up the children, as many of the women were consoling Daria aka Dashkiki.

I learned minimal information about my children's births and background before our first trip to meet them in Russia. Much emotion and time had been invested in the process prior to making that journey. Feeling a similar flood of emotions, I liken that first moment upon meeting the children to learning you are pregnant. It is also a point in life absent perfect guarantees of what happens in the coming months or years.

There certainly isn't a conclusive checklist or road map for adoption. Self-inquiry and doing the research ahead of time will enable you to step more preparedly into the process. Before I was ready to actually have or adopt children, I began researching domestic and international adoptions, as well as foster care. I was floored to learn of the millions of orphans around the world, and was compelled to pursue international adoption as most countries did not provide a foster system for the children.

I was drawn to adoption since I was a young person. I had a great interest in adopting a child from Africa due to the volume of need. Unlike some white Americans, having a child that looked like me was not a factor. In addition to the knowledge that children of color were at greater risk of being left behind, I learned that older children and sibling groups were likely to age out of orphanages. I initially met with a family friend who had started the non-profit adoption organization, Hope International; she was also an adoptive mom herself. I told her I was interested in learning about children who were at high-risk of not being adopted, such as an older child. She suggested a baby adoption for a first time parent due to the emotional and developmental challenges non-infant adoptees experience.

I left the meeting more informed, yet with even more questions, for the journey I was considering. I knew I wasn't quite ready to begin the process, but understood we would profile for an infant child when the time arrived. Studies led by psychologist, Marko Elovainio, suggest a higher predictability of aggressiveness and advanced behavioral challenges in non-infant adoptees, whereas the symptoms for babies are more somatic and internalized, such as anxiousness or withdrawal. I learned this through extensive research and reading during the following months. I wish I would have equally delved deeper into my feelings and what was going on in my inner world at that time. Why did I want to adopt, why wasn't I really ready yet, and would I ever be ready?

Within the year of that meeting, I received a phone call from the same agency wanting to tell me about a three-year-old sister and two-year-old brother in Russia. I was told that their biological mother was deceased. The girl would soon age out of the baby home (that is what they call orphanages for babies to toddler age). It was heartbreaking to imagine the siblings, all they knew of family, being separated. Remembering that non-infant children and sibling groups were in the category of higher risk of non-adoption, I knew the outlook for the children was increasingly concerning. I also knew that call was more than serendipitous.

EMOTIONAL INTELLIGENCE (EQ)

The phone call was life changing. While more subtle than what is now referred to as a "qualifying" life event, like getting married, loosing healthcare coverage, or moving, this moment was as poignant as love at first sight across a coffee shop. The ability to find balance between my heartstrings and pragmatism about what was best for my family, myself, and the orphans got increasingly more complicated. Although there were definitely times when I overthought something, finding symbiosis between my head and my heart was quite effective in the adoption decision process.

My background and training in mind-body work helped me to recalibrate, and notice the creep of anxiousness. The ability to listen to my own heart and to discern well crystalized when I actively acknowledged my instincts. In psychology, we refer to this as one's emotional intelligence (EQ). Someone with high EQ has keen self-awareness of the feeling in their heart, the thinking in their mind, and can integrate the two in a balanced way to make good choices and take action. Through the adoption process, I learned you don't just earn this high EQ badge in one day, it is like exercising, resting, and replenishing a muscle if you want peak performance.

L A B OR, PICKUP AND DELIVERY

The day will inevitably arrive when a child questions how or why you are their parent even though you don't share the same DNA. This may present itself in a variety of direct and indirect ways. Kids grow up with fairy tales, books, television shows, and movies in which family is most often the centerpiece. The modern world is becoming more alternative-family-friendly, but the traces of the Cleaver family run deep.

It wasn't until the day we were driving back from my son's birthday party at a park, that he said, "but I didn't come from your tummy." I'm pretty sure my breathing stopped and he could hear the roar of my heart pounding. How was this sweet and only 7-year old boy even thinking about this right after balloons, cake, obstacle courses, and a seat full of unopened gifts! I wanted to convince him that he came from love, but he was too bright, and knew there was more to it. That was true in a figurative sense, but he deserved the truth that his heart and mind were revealing they were ready to start hearing.

At the kids' request during the first year of adoption, I regularly read P.D. Eastman's book, "Are You My Mother?" The protagonist baby earthworm propositions a cow, a dog, a cat and a jumbo jet in search of his mother. I would tell the kids about the imaginary red kerchief I wore on my flight to Russia, just as the mother in the story wore as she flew to the nest, where baby and mama bird eventually united. All of the elements that needed to align in order for our adoption to be realized felt divine. Translating that to the kid's language meant, I had traveled over 30,000 miles back and forth, across three countries, to come and get *only* them.

Blood, genetics, gestation, labor and delivery are certainly differentiating factors between a biological mom and adoptive mom. What happens beyond this point, with the uniquely dealt cards, is true and *real* parenting. I'm thinking of nursing scrapes and bruises, sitting with them for hours until they fell asleep, only to return another hour when they woke up scared, appointment and meeting after meeting with doctors, therapists, teachers, and school officials, trying to garner a smile while cleaning up a sick mess, making a million mistakes, changing your schedule so they can spend time with a new friend or explore a new skill, holding them and their tears with each rejection and misstep along the way, and other varieties of terrifying, maddening, and odd tasks. I say that lightheartedly, as most real moms would.

The adoptive child needs to be granted years of space and patience to understand what a real mom means uniquely to themselves. Providing an adoptive child the truth (with appropriate timing), as hard as it is to hear, is boundless love. The children may not have gestated in my belly, but they are divine angels of serendipity. We couldn't have come as far as we have without humility, ruptures, repairs, the bare truth, and of course, laughter. Psychologist and writer on loving bravely, Alexandra Solomon, says a "willingness to stand honestly in our story takes guts… owning our core issues moves us from passive to active, and from victim to survivor, deepening our capacity to love."

WHILE YOU'RE WAITING...

Describe your unique story,

- What is your life like now, what world will your adoptive child be entering?

- When did you first begin thinking about having a child, and about adoption?

- What were your perceptions about adoption before now? And, how are they different post adoption decision?

- How will you feel when your child begins to wrestle with the idea of their adoption?

CHAPTER 4

REWIND, THE ADOPTION OPTION

There seemed to be birthday parties, often back to back, when my children were between the ages of six and eleven years old. While the kids bump into one another in a bounce house or ran wet and wildly around a spray park, the parents would casually chat with one another on the periphery of the party. This form of socializing was an abrupt change, a contrast from what I was used to as part of a double-income, no-kid couple. The conversation landscape changed from music, politics, and travel aspirations to the lists of the best schools, mutual friends, general gossip, and the weather.

All parents know the days that feel like survival of the fittest, some are longer than others. Ours were enduring at that time. Therefore, I loved the roller skating parties, where I could skate, (my favorite thing as a child), play and assist all of the kids. Admittedly, it was a bit of an escape from when I didn't agree to engage in the gossip about other parents, teachers, and coaches. Plus, I've heard I was one of the subjects of the gossip, for I had the kids that colored out of the lines.

Occasionally, there were individuals who wanted to know more upon hearing that we adopted two non-infant kids simultaneously. The softening of their hearts, the look in their eyes, the extension of their compassion were penetrating. Like others, they ask, "Why did you choose adoption," but their inquiry was deeper sourced. You can tell they've either considered adoption, may know someone who has, or they have experienced hardship. They knew the cost and gift of sacrifice, blood, sweat and tears.

One mom said, "you're a true saint." Empathy showed up inside of inquiry and listening. Her reflection back to me was something I could not see for myself at the time. Not only did it offer understanding, but it forged connection, which is becoming increasingly elusive in today's society. "You saved their lives," she continued. I never thought of myself as a saint in this way, or saving their lives. However, it's a common figurative statement made about adoptive parents, made by people, who I believe, understand the preciousness of life, and how things can change in an instant.

THE QUESTION OF WHY

The "why" behind one's decisions and actions rarely has a singular and simple response. Many factors, such as timing, past experiences, relationships, career, finances, and emotional needs, influence our thoughts and actions. Not too long ago, you were at the crossroads of a decision that would be forever life-changing. Let's take a look at some of the most common reasons people come to the decision of adoption.

According to the U.S. Census, 81.5 million Americans have considered adoption, and the most recent data reports an average of 119,000 adoptions occurring per year. You may know someone who has adopted, or admire those who have adopted. Natural childbirth may not have been an option for a variety of reasons. You want a family. You want to be closer on another level with your partner/spouse. You feel the abundance in your existing family, kids included, could enhance the love you share and benefit a child in need. You could be any of these people.

NATURAL CHILDBIRTH AND INFERTILITY

You may have arrived here in or from the heartache and fatigue of infertility. Adoption may have never been on your radar, but what has prevailed is an undying pull toward having a family. Women who have ever used infertility treatment are ten times more likely to have adopted, according to the U.S. Census.

One of my clients, Joann, lived large in her work and personal life. She had abundant energy and drive, climbing the corporate ladder, traveling across the nation for work, and the world for fun. She and her husband opened up the option of getting pregnant. After three years absent of becoming pregnant, she took stock of her life and health, and began fertility treatments, as starting a family was no longer a passive concept in their relationship. She was ready to "have" a baby!

Fast forward beyond numerous trips to the doctor's office, the rollercoaster of hormones and an unfortunate miscarriage, Joanna found herself in therapy contemplating what to do next amidst nursing the pain that was surfacing from her desire and efforts to become pregnant. It may seem illogical, but the experience of fertility can challenge one's self-worth, meaning in life, mortality, energy, and relationships (past and present). Joanne's fertility experience handicapped her joy and her hopes. She eventually decided to cease the fertility treatments. This indirectly created the space for her to face and reflect the deeper feelings that had bubbled to the surface. She has later reported that this pause offered her the time to redefine what motherhood truly meant for her in the narrative of her life, (which now includes an adopted baby girl).

RELATIONSHIP AND LIFESTYLE

Adoption may feel like the perfect choice for your life as a single or coupled woman. Single parents make up a third of foster care adoptions, up from an estimated half of one percent to four percent in the 1970s, according to the U.S. Department of Health and Human Services. Over nineteen percent of same-sex couples have at least one adopted child, according to the U.S. Census. "Research is showing that children raised by gay or lesbian couples show a lot of sensitivity, openness, and a freedom of biases, so there are birth parents who prefer placing children with them."

Other personal factors may contribute to adoption being an organic choice for you, such as your health circumstances present adoption as a safer or better alternative to pregnancy. You may also simply choose to become a parent without the experience of being pregnant. The phrase about one's "biological clock" ticking follows a young woman from her mid-twenties to mid-thirties. It is more metaphor than scientific, in fact, it can be interpreted as a baby panic or pressure for career women to have children. This phrase not only limited having children and families to natural childbirth, but also excluded men from the reproduction and family making conversation. The option of adoption disrupts the limited view of having a family. In fact, one out of every twenty-five families in the U.S. has an adopted child, according to the U.S. Census.

HUMANITY AND CONNECTION

You may have a solid foundation of family support and structure that has enabled you to explore and experience life. You may have a history of service and volunteering, exercising a muscle that has increased strength to take on more. You may have experienced an upbringing with abundant love and support that you didn't even realize the extent of until you were an adult and witnessed struggle in the world. Perhaps, you were a foster or adopted kid, and you want to give back. You understand first-hand what it is like to live with unanswered questions, stigma, and needs.

Perhaps, you grew up seeing the commercials of children of hunger, poverty, war, abuse, or deprivation. The plight of children in the foster and adoption systems is overwhelmingly challenging, and growing. It can be non-productive to allow our concern and worries for these children to keep us up at night, and ultimately disrupt our family and work lives. Those individuals who have been brought to their knees with the overwhelming empathy - for those in need - may simply not be able to deny the pull toward adoption as a way to do something about it, a way to make a difference in the world.

I was drawn to adoption for years as I couldn't shake the fact that millions of children were growing up homeless and without the support that having a family can provide. At the same time, I wasn't in a position to pursue adoption until I had a greater sense of maturity, selflessness, and resources. Through my own reflective practice, I uncovered my guilt about the unearned privilege I possess being born into middle-class, white America. It allowed me to witness the pain and need from a distance. My unearned white privilege allows me to make a donation, feel better about myself, and move on with my day. That is not enough for myself.

During my time of research and self-inquiry, I spoke to friends and family members about the possibility of adoption. It was difficult for many people to relate to my choice of adoption in place of natural childbirth. I went to one of my most respected and beloved sources, my mother-in-law. She was a child-development expert, and was one of the first Montessori trainers in Texas. I recall her words to me, "don't adopt for only humanitarian reasons."

She challenged me to find the deeper pull I had toward adoption. I eventually realized that through the decision process and the adoption, I found the unexpected home for my quiet strength, patience, and kindness that was a misfit in some of life's other endeavors. I realized it wasn't simply for humanitarian reasons; there was and is an inner mama bear (as my kids have called it) that wanted to and had the ability to share, give, and experience love. It might have been my life, (and theirs), that was proverbially saved by the treasure of adoption.

WHILE YOU'RE WAITING...

What is the true essence of your pull towards adoption?

Too often, we get caught up in societal and familial self-imposed expectations and narratives. There are parts of your story that are continually left unsaid, and there are parts of it that are beyond our immediate awareness. Explore the following questions as you establish a contemplative practice in your life, for it will pay dividends beyond finding greater clarity in your adoption decision.

- What motivated you to order/pick up this book?
- Which of the events in your life played a crucial part in bringing you to the consideration of adoption?
- What do you think makes you suited for adoption? What would others say makes you suited?
- What are you looking most forward to in the idea of becoming an adoptive parent? Which aspect is most exciting to you? What are your fears?

CHAPTER 5

REJECTION ON GOTCHA DAY

Although the final van ride from St. Petersburg to the orphanage was five hours across every color of grey imaginable, I was too excited about getting the kids and bringing them home to think about anything that could go wrong. Sergei, my designated driver for all things Russian adoption, didn't speak much English. I imagined him coming from a large family of siblings, and a devoted father. He efficiently took care of navigation and ensuring we got to every visit, ministry appointment, and meetings that we would never have been able to find in Tikhvin and St. Petersburg.

At this point in the journey, rounds of paperwork, appointments, and meetings had occurred to make the adoption possible. I knew from the prior visit that there wasn't anything I could do more of on the remote road to Tikhvin. The hollow van felt like being inside a dried up soda can found on the side of the street. The best way to avoid getting carsick was to lay down on the seat of one of the three rows. Perhaps, it was a surrendering to the unknown, the calm before the sweet storm.

I closed my eyes and imagined what the day had been like for the children. I hoped they were as happy as the last time I saw them. I thought about their fantastic smiles as they both waved goodbye from the little classroom window. You've seen the image of an adorable child looking out a window, with the innocent look of longing mixed with the promise of forever love. In fact, you likely have images in your head now of what it will be like to hold your adoptive child in your arms as his or her eyes lock onto yours.

The fading of that window visual over time allowed me to remember it the way I wanted. I don't think that robbed the kids of what it was truly like for them. For, I wondered about it during the months before I would see them again. I wasn't aware of what they had been told about us and the change coming in their lives. I know I saw a longing in their eyes, likely tied to the familiar feeling of abandonment that they would not be able to name.

I felt a fusion of nervousness, anticipation and joy upon entering the orphanage that day, imagining bounds of excitement, two smiling kids running down the hallway and into my arms, possibly tackled, finally, forever! That feeling was put to rest immediately by hearing the loudest screams of a child you could ever imagine, the blood curling kind. My heart ached for the pain I heard in the cries the moment right before I realized it was my daughter. Like a heartbreaking broken record, she kept repeating "I don't want to go! I don't want to go! I don't want to go!" With her Russian beat red face, she had worked herself into a fit, and was barely consolable. Several of the caretakers huddled around her with soothing words, hugging and holding her.

Per the instructions, I had brought both kids a backpack with a change of clothes. One of the rules was that the kids were not to leave with anything from the orphanage than what they had been given from outside the orphanage. Both of the kids had the stuffed animals I had brought them at the last visit. A koala bear and a monkey, with long arms that could clasp around their necks. While focused on resolving my daughter's distress, my son had changed his clothes, wrapped the monkey around his neck and put on his backpack. He looked at me, ready to go! This was an encouraging sign of resilience and adaptation in a child that both he and his sister have exhibited in different ways and at different times over the years.

DEFENSIVE STRATEGIES

I looked over at his sister, still in her pajamas and soaked hair from the fit of tears. That day did not go as I had dreamed. I don't know any parent who would say things have gone exactly as they expected. Whether it's the best-laid plans that are inverted, or ignorance is bliss, it is helpful to consider how you feel when life throws you the curveball, serves you lemons and leaves you in its dust. Different people respond in different ways when they don't get what they want, or when their position, abilities, values, beliefs, needs or desires are questioned. It's no wonder defensiveness sets in when you add fatigue, work demands, or unresolved past hurts. I could have taken my daughter's screams and initial rejection as an affirmation of my fears about being a good enough future parent, setting off an arsenal of unhelpful defenses. Having addressed issues of inadequacy through a reflective process will build your resilience for the inevitable parenting moments that question your entire being.

The contemplative practice introduced in Chapter One provides a framework for reflecting on how you typically handle things not going as planned or desired, being wrong, or being wronged. Has anyone told you, "you're just being defensive?" Well, is there a chance you were? Not all defense mechanisms are maladaptive. Your defenses have likely protected you in a harmful or unhealthy situation, while at other times, have made things more difficult for you. Coping with inner conflict, especially those with deep roots from the past, relies on the subconscious employing one of the many defenses mechanisms.

Defenses vary, depending on the circumstances and one's internal psyche and structural development. In some instances, one reaction may be a denial of what is happening, even subconsciously hoping the problem will disappear, dissipate. Other times, we launch into blaming someone else. Exerting control over another is an example of more complex defense, one that is neurotic in nature, compared to an adaptive defense, like humor or channeling our instincts or reactions into something positive. A reaction such as anger, often ill-considered a negative emotion, can be productively alerting us that something may not be a right fit for us, and can actually be the catalyst for change. Recognizing the ways in which your defense strategies surface is seriously important in parenting any child as it has a powerful potential to affect their developing selves.

COPING SKILLS

Other times, we employ coping strategies, such as a "get it done" mode when life throws a curveball. Sublimating our energy in that way can be productive, one just needs to be careful that it doesn't serve as a complete distraction from unmet needs or root causes of problems. The concept of mindset was developed by

Stanford psychologist and researcher, Carol Dweck. She posits that a person may have a fixed or growth mindset, orienting the way they handle situations. A parent with a *growth* mindset does not see failure in imperfection or in a day taking the turn for the worse. They cope by employing effort, will, hope, and belief.

FLEXIBILITY VERSUS PERFECTION

Francis was one of my first patients at a women's eating disorder treatment center. The relationship between women and food often has layers of struggles with the loss of control in one's life, relationships, school, or work. The intake or lack of food can be controlled by the patient in a way that they feel or think they cannot control other areas of life. Note, this is not the singular predictor of an eating disorder, yet it played a significant role in Francis' eating disorder almost fatally succeeding.

Francis would eat one time per day in a specific way: alone, and at night. This allowed for perfect execution of her ritual in lining up the individual foods she believed were safe and would keep her alive and brutally underweight. The precision of the order and quantity of foods matched the perceived perfection in the number on her scale. This ritual could not be disrupted by social outings with friends or family; she would sacrifice any of that in order to sustain the perfection she believed she was creating. The time in which this ritual would get rattled by a social engagement, a work obligation, or family need caused severe anxiety. Yet, those responses also provided a window into a place inside of her heart that needed to be healed, or a story that needed to be heard.

Perfection is elusive and gives a false and temporary promise in preventing things from going wrong. Other responsibilities and people important to us can feel neglected when so much focus and attention is put into perfecting one aspect of our lives. Francis' case is extreme. On a lighter note, the occasional spill on the couch or rug, the unexpected call from school with a high fever, or being late due to a child's meltdown that occurs right as you all are walking out the door can throw the day completely off - if our mindset allows it. The spiral of discontent can be averted by reflecting now on the roots of perfection, what purpose it is serving, what you're willing to let go of, and how to cope when things don't go your way.

STIGMA AND SOCIAL LIFE

Besides the daily surprises, obstacles, and last-minute changes that come with parenting, especially high need children, other subtleties need to be considered as an adoptive parent. If you are one to get preoccupied or bothered by what other people, couples, and families are doing or have, especially in comparison to yourself, it's important to know that adoption may add to that distress. It's helpful to consider how your life will change relative to the status quo. Considering how you like to spend your time, your values, and the qualities in interpersonal relationships you desire are all helpful in this sense. Reflecting on how satisfied you are in that area of your life may highlight for you some deficiency or affirm a solid sense of contentment.

Adoption is slowly becoming more normalized. As an adoptive parent, you will inevitably, be presented with a situation where someone doesn't understand the complexities, or worse, may discriminate against you or your child. A negative stigma of adoption, held by self or offered by others, can challenge one's affliction with perfectionism that resides in their subconscious. Getting clear about your thoughts and understanding of adoption as a social, cultural, economic, and global health priority is a necessity. The ability to stay in alignment with your values in these moments, and to sustain life's challenges in parenting adoptive children requires a solid level of sweat equity on your part.

WHILE YOU'RE WAITING...

How do you react when things don't go as planned?

- What image or dream comes to mind when you think about your potential future adopted child and yourself?
- Think about the status quo in your life now. How do you anticipate that changing upon becoming a parent?
- How do you handle disturbances in your schedule, to-do's, bed-time, or even watching your favorite show?
- How do you cope with stress? What is your most effective coping strategy?

- What messages did you receive about people and/ or families that are different than yours? Describe if/what have you heard or experienced relative to a stigma around adoption, and if/how that may be a challenge for you or your family.

CHAPTER 6

(BAD) ADVICE FROM A RUSSIAN SOCIAL WORKER

The only way I knew what Daria was screaming on Gotcha Day was due to our translator. Natalia, a former teacher during the collapse of the Soviet Union, lived alone and loved reading. The end of the Soviet Union brought hopes of the end of censorship on books. She explained that she still couldn't get the full version of books that made her simple life more colorful. There are two main publishing houses, the king and queen of publishing in Russia. They scrutinize every manuscript before they agree to publish. The ones that make it through are abridged beyond recognition. We brought Natalia books on each trip from the United States, such as Doctor Shivago, Notre Dame de Fleurs, Anna Kareinam, Crime and Punishment, and The Brothers of Karamazov. The rare smile on a face that had seen so much oppression over the years was more enjoyable than the golubtsy, (the homemade cabbage casserole she gave us to express her gratitude).

"Gotcha Day" is the term used in the adoption world for when a child joins the family. As you now know, our Gotcha Day at the orphanage was highly charged beyond Daria's tears, I imagine the orphanage caregivers assumed somewhat of a parental role for the children, and they were facing their own grief saying goodbye to the kids. Understandably, Daria didn't want to leave her home and family that consisted of the staff and the other kids. She was the oldest child at the orphanage; I had watched her lead the rest of them in play earlier that summer. "Dashki," the caregivers would say in an authoritative tone as they helped her finish getting dressed and encouraged her to get ready complete the final day at the orphanage. The kids were traumatized with leaving, making it understandable as to why they weren't jumping in my arms with joy.

VULNERABILITY

I'm not sure if Daria's tears had finished or the well dried up at that point, but she acquiesced with a quiet calm that replaced the screams. Alex must have learned early to fly under the radar when needed - as he continued to wait quietly. He simply followed the lead of myself or the Russian social worker, Svletlanna, who was assisting us through the transition from the orphanage to the van. The goodbyes were a gut-wrenching blur. As Svletlanna and I were securing the kids in their seats, my fingers began to tingle and go numb, and my head filled with heat although it was bitter cold and dark outside.

I was overwhelmed with the hours of screaming and tears, and with helping the precious children who had been deprived of so much in comparison to what American babies and toddlers are accustomed. Then abruptly, my arm snapped. It was the brutal grip of Svletlanna's hand, "don't ever let them see you cry." I looked into her piercing eyes, and again, as if it would be a death sentence, "don't ever let them see you cry." I didn't need Natalia's translation this time.

Carsickness out of the way early, the long bumpy van ride through the night was surreal. I was sitting on that same bench seat with my two children. I likened it to going into labor. Alex eventually fell asleep, whereas Daria sat straight up watching everything. Her beautiful blue eyes almost doubled in size as she saw the lights of St. Petersburg approach. I automatically transitioned into the role of protector and mom once we arrived in St. Petersburg late that night.

HUMAN CAPITAL

Any ability to ask for help or to express my feelings was lost in the constant state of averting disaster, the threat of "don't ever let them see you cry," and the "lump in my throat" that got stuck there (for years) upon that pivotal moment back at the van. There is no glory in martyrdom, in fact, it eventually keeps those who love you furthest away. I didn't need to find humility as I never professed to know all I needed to know, in fact, I often didn't know what I needed.

Turns out, it actually does take a village. We were in survival mode the first two years. It was natural for parents who have been through similar experiences with a high need infant or child were the people who understood, they were relentless in their gestures of support. One of the most valuable expressions of help I received was from a best friend, a single-adoptive mom, taking an entire week off of work to help me with "anything" I needed. She came to the house each day, doing anything from helping with the kids, putting furniture together, and running to the store for everything we forgot. My mother-in-law also came over frequently for a few hours at a time, and was tremendously helpful in her advice and playful attention to the kids.

There was a magical afternoon in which the kids' aunt, uncle and three cousins came to the house to visit. Any opportunity my kids had to be around other children seemed to be the most enjoyable time for them. This made sense given their previous life consisted of living with over twenty kids day and night. The cousins were a little older and had likely been coached by their parents on how to be open and flexible with our kids. They probably didn't realize they would convert into figures to climb upon and chase around the yard. Their aunt would hold the kids in her lap, and their uncle gave limitless bear hugs. That afternoon left an imprint on the kids, helping us to further establish a base of security for them.

This visit was a perfect example of the divine in simplicity and family. However, minimizing stimuli by not changing the environment for the first few months home prevents further activation of their heightened nervous system. There is too much of a good thing in including others in your child's first six months home. This is a critical period of attachment and bonding, which will be discussed in Chapter Seven.

Expanding beyond family, friends can be of invaluable support by simply listening, offering perspective, and laughs. It's quite lovely when a friend brings the outer world to you when you are so buried and can't see the forest through the trees. Something I wished I would have asked of my friends was to sit with my kids, thus freeing me up to take care of other tasks. Of course, stealing me away for a meal or coffee, if the stars aligned, was wonderful. I suggest you assume your friends and family want to help, but don't know how to do so.

Another potential source of support and compassion is your place of work, if that applies to you. I was fortunate to work for a company who valued family and flexibility. Nurturing your relationships at work, establishing communication and expectations, will pay dividends as you find yourself in new circumstances and events you simply will not be able to predict.

FINANCIAL HEALTH

This chapter has largely been about support and resources in friendly terms of human capital. The status of your financial state is an important to factor in as you assess and get resourced for adoption. For the seventh year in a row, the American Psychological Association's annual *Stress in America* survey found that money is the top source of stress for American adults. More than a quarter of Americans say they feel stressed about money most or all of the time. Tackling your financial to do list as much as possible prior to adoption homecoming day is easier said than done, and entirely necessary. You likey won't have the time for it during the first year of adoption. Putting your bills on autopay is an example of identifying ways to simplify your life, especially if left neglected, could be costly. You will need any free time you can find.

ASKING FOR HELP

I worked at a counseling center for teen moms, where childcare services were provided while the young women participate in therapy, schoolwork, and job skills development. Lisa, one of the teen moms, was wholeheartedly committed to the program, but it was like pushing a rock up a hill with each day for her. One day she arrived as normal, after four bus stops and rain in traffic. She delivered her baby to the nursery so she could begin her day only to learn that the agency could not allow the child to stay with the fever and cold symptoms she presented. Lisa had to pack up her things, get back onto another hour-plus bus ride to the room she rented from a friend.

In therapy, Lisa and I were working on the load of responsibilities she had as a teen mom, the socio-economic challenges increased by having a baby, the turmoil of her relationship with the father of her baby, and her own mother. Lisa returned to the center the following week after her baby's fever had dissipated. In therapy, we explored the fatigue and shame that she was feeling from the prior week's incident. "They must think I'm a terrible mom for not knowing my baby was ill," she cried. This false sense of separation she was feeling from others is a common experience I witness in many of my clients, creating much internal suffering.

Lisa and I worked with her feelings of isolation, her declining health, and on finding the pause between the cycle of arising stress and dissolving pain. She uncovered her fears and shame while remembering the strength and resolve that had originally brought her to our program. She wanted her diploma, and to find a stable job in order to support her baby and herself. We practiced "the ask," word for word together until she found truth in her vulnerability. She asked her mother and the estranged father of her child for help so she could complete the program. Despite the past hurt in these relationships, a childcare schedule had been agreed to within a week. Fast forward, Lisa has graduated from the program, earned her GED, and has found employment. Asking for help also served as an opportunity for a renewed connection between Lisa, her baby and her family.

WHILE YOU'RE WAITING...

How do you ask for help?

The unfriendly instruction of "don't ever let them see you cry" was the least helpful advice I may have ever received. While quantifying resources and support is important, evaluating whether or not you are comfortable in receiving and asking for support will help you further paint how those first few years will look as an adoptive parent. Even when you say it out loud, yes most of us do, "what have I gotten myself into here," to what degree will you be willing to roll up your sleeves, get down at knee level with your child and work through the challenge together? Brene Brown taught us that "vulnerability sounds like truth and feels like courage. Truth and courage aren't always comfortable, but they're never weakness." Consider your comfort in humility, and how courageous you are willing to be.

- Describe the village, if any, you had as a child. Who would your village consist of as an adoptive parent, consider if/how it expands beyond immediate family?

- Time is precious, yes everyone is busy, how will you ask them for help?

- What is your employment situation? What is your dream employment situation once you are an adoptive parent? What kind of support do you anticipate needing from your work (i.e. Flex scheduling, work from home, et cetera)?

- On a blank page, draw your core family with your future adopted kid(s). Then sketch and list the human capital and outside support that will make up your village.

CHAPTER 7

BE WELL, PARENT WELL

The night we arrived at the hotel in St. Petersburg from the orphanage began with a bath. Entering a new building meant more people, more space, more lights, more stairs, more everything added to the kids' stress hormones and confusion. The neurobiological effect with trauma can hinder the brain's ability to process incoming senses. Children of neglect may have learned to shut off unnecessary brain functions in order to survive. My four year old daughter and three year old son spoke full Russian, and not a bit of English. This compounded the mystery of what they were feeling or needing. Without knowing the degree to which they may have been experiencing fear or stress, it was crucial that I managed external stimuli and introduced things gradually and tenderly with them.

Not only did a nighttime bath seem like the normal thing to do, placing them in the confines of a smaller space, like a tub, would be calming to their nervous system. I'll never forget the smiles on their faces as they played with the bars of soap and tiny tubes of bubbles. They didn't notice the startling transformation of the clear bathwater changing to a murky brown color as days of orphanage dust and dirt washed off of their skin.

The lost chance to shower myself that night began a decline of self-care in parenting two high-need, spirited children. From the moment I dried them off, for at least the next six months, (although, I did shower the next morning while they finally slept), I was on heightened alert and constant guard of their safety. Children from the adoption system, and often the foster system, have not had exposure to the normal things in our lives such as scissors, dinner knives, stairs, pens, or power outlets. I immediately tended to the kids as they'd scurry around the room, attempting to play with and climb on what they could.

Ironically, showers became my guilty pleasure, the singular source of time alone. I'd tap into the self-care and breathing at full capacity I had taught so often in the yoga room. Exercising, long runs, coffee mornings, and sleeping in on Saturday became increasingly elusive. Self-care nourishes and replenishes what we need and want to do in life, and how we show up for it. Self-care happens in many ways in addition to what and how we eat, and the quality and quantity of our sleep. My training at The Institute for Integrative Nutrition in New York refers to this as "primary foods," which are nonfood sources of nourishment, such as career, relationships, physical activity, and spirituality. One way to understand this is truly noticing how the absence of sleep, love, or power drives a desire for excess food or meaningless stimuli. Just like the absence of vitamins and nutrients in our diets, we can become malnourished by deficiencies in the other areas of life that feed our heart and minds.

YOU LOOK TIRED

I think people mean well when they say, "you look tired." Again, for the most part, they don't know what to do to support you; I want to believe it is a way for them to express care or concern. I certainly was exhausted, that is until I took the reins back on my health. The first step was choosing to not ignore how differently I felt compared to the past, and to consider what primary food areas of my life needed attention. None of us are completely above depletion or misfiring on self-care; it's a huge wake-up call the moment it affects those we love. As an adoptive parent, I recognized I wanted to show up better for myself, my family, and my work.

One of the other adoptive parents I worked with at a counseling private practice was struggling with her diet habits during the adoption journey. She often did not have time to eat, or would just eat whatever was available, which led to junk food, crunchy snacks, and alcohol. She eventually realized the emotional connection as she reconciled her relationship with food and drinking. Utilizing the principles of mindful eating, Angie realized she was using food as comfort, and in a punitive way as she felt an increasing lack of control over her schedule and intimacy with her spouse. Once she reflected on her satisfaction with the different aspects of her life, and truly listened to what her eating behaviors were telling her, she was able to catch herself in those moments where she wanted to escape into the habit of checking out and eating mindlessly. Angie found a sense of authority over her self-care, which empowered her to find the same in other areas of her life.

Clients often refer to the obstacles of time management and balancing all of the personal and professional commitments they've made. Add emotions and desires to that mix, and inevitably what you need the most in self-care falls by the wayside. You can interrupt this downward spiral by maintaining your health and well-being as a priority and life source for your family.

The *Wheel of Life* is often used in personal development as a way for one to gauge their satisfaction in primary elements of life, such as family, career, spirituality, finances, intellect, joy, creativity, and health and fitness. As you were making the decision to become an adoptive parent, you were responding to a need, desire, imbalance or question about life. Take a moment to rate your level of satisfaction (1-being not satisfied at all to 5-being extremely satisfied) with each category. Mark each spoke of the wheel, from zero at the center to five at the edge, then connect the dots to capture a visual of how balanced your life is. There is certainly not a perfect picture expected here, but it can reveal areas of life in which you are putting more effort into and some that are not getting as much attention as they may need.

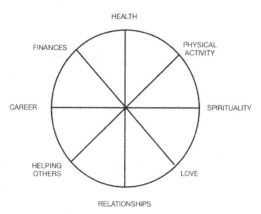

TOO BUSY FOR JOY

The biology of our bodies is quite impressive, permitting survival in extreme conditions. Physical signs of a 911 call to the self-care line may be consistent stiffness or aches in your bones and body, difficulty falling asleep, procrastination, and impatience. Being abrupt and short with kids are often signs of fatigue or feeling overwhelmed. At one time, being busy suggested an aura of importance about a person. I've often witnessed how a client's busy-ness helps them avoid other areas of their lives, such as joy and pleasure.

Joy is an extraordinarily gratifying emotion, yet can be quite vulnerable to experience. Sheer joy can surface in the authenticity of a smile from another, helping someone, expressing your creativity or interests freely, and many other ways. Joy fills our bodies with energy, can make us scream with delight, reach out to others, and actually relax. While all of these are lovely, they can also feel risky. Joy is visceral, cannot be purchased, and is unlike happiness as it is not tied to a result or outcome. To feel joy means risking disappointment, rejection or embarrassment if others cannot meet our expectations for hope, companionship or love. For some people, these risks are too high, and they avoid joy purposely, or often without even realizing they are doing so.

Often people cover joy with other emotions that ride along with thoughts designed to inhibit pleasure. People may instead experience shame and unworthiness: "I don't deserve to feel happy." Or fear: "This is going to end anyway; why feel it at all?" Or guilt: "I shouldn't express such joy in front of others who do not have the privilege to feel the same way."

Early experiences in our families can feed the tremendous joy of innocence, or teach us that joy is fleeting and will vanish as quickly as it arrived. For some, joy becomes dangerous, something to avoid at all costs – even if it's the more pleasant route. I'm curious how much joy contributes to the quality of your life, and if the absence of it is more psychologically expensive. There is a responsibility to consider the child in this equation now that you have decided to become a parent. The joy a family experiences is a result of effort, compassion, care and time. Furthermore, how a parent meets their own expectations of joy can intersect with the wish for the ideal family, the one with the white picket fence.

The dream of having a family can displace one's expectations of a perfect picture family unintentionally onto the children. This can rob the child of the freedom of an organic childhood experience as they unknowingly try to fit into the role they've been cast in the parent's crafted movie. The child becomes more of an object than human, which is further precarious for an adoptive child who is already pushing a rock up the proverbial hill of social and emotional development. Intentionally crowding out the things in life that are not essential, and do not bring you joy is especially important in managing the compassion fatigue of being a caregiver to a high need child.

WHILE YOU'RE WAITING...

How do you take care of yourself?

One way to avoid self-care tipping the scale to the dark side is expressing what you need from loved ones, whether it be time, space, closeness or support. Taking extremely good care of yourself is, in fact, taking good care of your loved ones, for you can be stronger, more energetic and more nourishing for them when your needs are met.

- How do you define self-care? In what ways do you practice it?

- To what degree do you put others needs in place of yours?

- How often do you snap back at someone? To what degree have your ruminated or felt shame about your action after the fact?

- How have you (figuratively) made room in your life for children? How will your schedule need to change?

- Have you made a bucket list? How do you cultivate joy in your life now?

- Consider your physical health necessities. How are you translating exercise and health priorities into action?

- Is work, education or personal development a high priority in your life? Consider how having an adoptive child fits into your career goals.

- Consider the ways in which being busy is or has been an identity of yours, and how will having an adopted child contribute to that real or perceived busy-ness.

CHAPTER 8

LOVING A HURT CHILD

We headed for the Moscow airport on the kids' final day in Russia. By that time, the excitement had been replaced by the reality of the complexities in adopting non-infant, non-English speaking orphaned children. The three of us were running on empty. The prior ten-days since leaving the orphanage consisted of bundling layers of clothes for the bitter winter weather, the overnight train ride to Moscow, doctor's visits and various appointments. One of the most surreal appointments was getting the children's photos done for their Russian passport. We were taken down a neighborhood street, and then walked down an alley into a barren warehouse. We were there for all of ten-minutes, the efficiency was appreciated, but I've never been able to shake how things could have gone badly in an instant.

All of the administrative tasks that needed to be done in Russia, plus the weather, didn't allow for much playtime. The three of us would march up and down the stairs of the hotel as they would try to repeat my counting numbers with their steps. We'd also climb and descend stairs to the rhythm of the alphabet. They were amazing, being shuffled all around by this stranger, me, while they were accustomed to staying in one confined place all day, all night. The children were beginning to get comfortable and would allow me to hold them and sit in my lap. However, there were times that I would look over at them and see the utter fear in their eyes.

The kids fell asleep once we boarded the plane headed to Frankfurt. Relief washed over me. I could finally take a breath, and gather myself and my thoughts a bit. However, the optimism I had about the flight was squandered once we settled into our seats on the flight from Frankfurt to Dallas. Alex's quiet calm and deference to his sister I first saw at the orphanage had expired into an eight-hour heartbreaking, gut-wrenching meltdown. He was inconsolable despite all the creative efforts the flight attendants and I could summon.

I tried marching the aisles with him as he so enjoyed it earlier that week. Being handed pizza ignited his screams; never in the history of mankind has a child launched an ice cream sundae across an airplane. After exhausting all of the toys, books, crafts I packed for the plane ride, I took him into the bathroom, in hopes that a contained environment would feel more secure to him. The crying continued, while Daria's eyes, wide open, may not have blinked at all. Meanwhile, the nearby passengers' compassion turned to frustration and disdain. It took me years to understand the kids and I were experiencing a trauma on that plane ride home.

This experience was layered for the kids who had already suffered trauma with being orphaned. We now know, through research and neuroscience, that a newborn child and infant can experience the trauma around them despite not being able to understand it. The field of neuropsychology has only recently been able to find evidence that there can be visual, (simply what a baby may see), trauma at less than one year of birth. Knowledge and preparation increases the potential for a child of trauma to have a higher quality of life, one that can be open to giving and receiving love in time.

The brain and nervous system of a child who has come from a difficult background are in confusion and underdeveloped. The duality of the child's experience is that bad things happened, and good things that were supposed to happen - did not. The fear, anger, and frustration can affect their biology, beliefs, and behavior. Of course, not all adoptive children come from a high risk background, and not all children that come from a high risk background have significant developmental delays. A parent must be willing to endure the rollercoaster of acceptance and rejection from a hurt child - for as little or long as it takes to establish trust.

THE IMPORTANCE OF ATTACHMENT

The bonding that takes place between an infant and their primary caregiver has been found as one of the most critical elements in a child's development. This bonding, in the first pivotal three years of life, not only includes uninterrupted periods of holding and affection, but also direct eye contact; the chance for the child to find that connection and security in the loving gaze. The absence of this bonding may precipitate social and emotional delays, withdrawn behavior and minimally seeking comfort when distressed. Enduring patterns or the degree of pervasiveness are considered in how much support or clinical intervention a child may need. Fortunately, vast knowledge and trained individuals exist to work with the adoptive families on mending the wounds of these early years.

Whether it is that bad things happened, or good things did not happen in their past, the child's sense of security is shattered, leaving them feeling scared and helpless. Attachment Theory, based largely on the work of psychologists John Bowlby and Mary Ainsworth, is rooted in the correlation between one's level of emotional health, behaviors, and their experience with her/his primary caregiver. Negative symptoms in an attachment disorder may range from depressive and withdrawn behavior to exaggerated disinhibition. Despite the instability, distrust, sensory issues and behavioral challenges, clinical diagnosis is rare.

In many cases, the adopted child is at a different stage of social and/or emotional development than his or her peers. While the emotional security, character and traits have been much attributed by the very early years, human growth and development occurs in stages and can offer hope. Although my kids looked like and presented like the biological kids of our friends and family, they were on a unique and separate trajectory. This understanding allowed for a reset of expectations, which was incredibly helpful. I began to notice the gap, in the development trajectory, was narrowing over time. Today it is barely existent.

Earlier, I wrote about the visual of the children waving goodbye from the orphanage window with compassion for the possibility of how it may have felt for them experiencing being left again. It is much to expect a child to comprehend or verbally express the range of emotions their body is experiencing in a moment like that. It's traumatic for a child to be left by their parent or primary caregiver, and my departure may have triggered unconscious negative memories of pain, abandonment, loss, or even a threatening circumstance. We won't ever know for sure, and that is why it is crucial to develop attuned parenting, and empathy around the possibility of past hurt. The reverberations of an early life trauma have the power to endure or surface in later behavior and relationships. The ability to believe in and act on the possibility that the children also felt a sense of love and warmth looking out that window, can be wildly powerful in living with trauma. Returning to that possibility, and nurturing it in moments of difficulty were often what pulled me off the edge of hopelessness.

YOU CAN'T REWRITE THEIR EARLY LIFE EXPERIENCE

I sought the input and support from a brilliant psychotherapist after the first six months of the kids being home. We were struggling, all of us. It had been enough time for me to notice the patterns in the children's behavior and emotions. I hoped for a deeper understanding of what the kids were experiencing and new ideas on how to help them. In hindsight, I would have interviewed therapists before the adoption was final. This would have provided a head start with counseling the support of the kids through their distress from the beginning.

The kids' behavior and emotions of fear, anger, and frustration were largely informed by their early life trauma, and this tremendous disruption in their lives of being adopted. I realized my sadness for them was taking over my heart. I was experiencing compassion fatigue and vicarious trauma. Researchers have identified personality characteristics in their interest in understanding compassion, empathy, and altruism. The Santa Clara Brief Compassion Scale was developed based on the work of Sprecher and Fehr. They define compassionate love as an "attitude toward other(s), either close others or strangers of all of humanity; containing feelings, cognitions, and behaviors that are focused on caring, concern, tenderness, and an orientation toward supporting, helping, and understanding the other(s)." Safe to assume, I tip the scale on this one.

The secondary trauma in witnessing and parenting the children's struggles challenged my impenetrable commitment to their well-being and happiness.

The day my therapist told me, "you can't make up for their early life experience. You can't change that time for them" helped relieve the grip of that responsibility and the guilt I was carrying for their biological parents. I began to own more clearly that I could only affect their life in the present moment, and going forward. While I am a real mom, being an adoptive parent prioritizes the needs of the child such that their experience does not look exactly like their peers. The hope is based on the potential to rebuild their emotional and developmental foundation, and break the cycle of traces of insecure or avoidant tendencies based on their early life experiences. I realized increased knowledge, patience with them and myself, asking for support, and not crumbling in a crisis would enable me to disrupt the negative trajectory of behavioral and mental health issues.

WHILE YOU'RE WAITING...

What can you do to become more informed about ways to cultivate attachment with your soon to be adopted child?

- What more can you find out about your future adoptive child's culture, development and background?

- If needed, consider how you are you prepared to adjust your parenting expectations to the child's developmental age, rather than their chronological age?
- How might you adjust the integration of your adoptive child into your home and with family and friends in consideration of stimuli overwhelm?

Much of what I write about in this book can certainly be experienced by families with biological children, as well as adoptive parents. You have or will participate in adoptive parenting classes, specifically related to more fully grasping the realm of trauma, and the potential effects on the brain, behavior, and development. An infant who receives sensitive and responsive care from their primary caregiver will likely form a sense of security and a feeling of being loved and valued. I believe an adoptive parent's role is to feel compassion, express humility in the unknown, and offer the children grace in strange moments and safety in the darkness.

CHAPTER 9

RESILIENCE, FRAGILITY AND LOVE

As the plane approached the airport, I began organizing how I would gather each of the carry-on bags and keep the children with me as we exited the plane. Many people walked by with disapproving looks until an angel appeared – really it was just another mom who "got it" – and helped me with the carry-ons and the kids through the jetway. Alex's distress continued as we moved through customs, immigration, and baggage claim. My hands were full, protecting the kids from going in two directions as I watched my large suitcase carried off into a secured area not to be seen again for three days. That would end up being irrelevant as I didn't have a chance to unpack it for a month.

My husband and his mom had been waiting on the other side of security for I'm sure what felt like a painfully long time. They may have had the same image of the kids gleefully running into their arms, but they were likely experiencing concern by this point. I wondered if they could hear my son's screams on the other side of security as we got closer to the exit. I was carrying him and his tears, while holding Daria's hand. I was completely overwhelmed with relief and love to see my husband and mother-in-law when I walked through the double doors. Unexpectedly, I also had mixed emotions that flooded my head with heat. My finger and hands tingled and went numb again, then the commands "don't ever let them see you cry" rang through my head. I handed Alex to my husband, placed Daria's hand in her grandmother's hand, and immediately walked in the other direction until I found a nook in the hallway and doubled over in sweat and my own tears. Do I make a run for it?

As real parents do, I gathered myself within the same few minutes and found the four of them waiting silently. Their eyes were wide with disbelief, wondering what to do next, what have we done, and where are we. Just like other insurmountable experiences you've had in your life, you most often take it one step at a time. So, we put the kids in the car and drove home.

My husband and I had been together for over seven years. We had been enjoying the freedom that growing careers and childless couples have. He was very supportive of my draw toward adoption. We were originally told that marital status would not be a factor, but that changed, like many things did in the process. We scheduled a date downtown to get married earlier in the year of the adoption. I remember picking him up at his office, the nervous jokes, and the odd feeling sitting across the desk from the justice of the peace. This wasn't quite how either of us imagined our wedding day. We didn't have any idea what the next five years were going to be like, but we believed we were going down the right path, the one that felt right.

I can only imagine the range of things that may have gone through my husband's mind while I was in Russia gathering and bringing the kids home. He could partially formulate an image because we had gone together to meet the kids earlier that year. He couldn't go on this trip due to work demands. This inadvertently was the beginning of our separateness in roles. Our situation fell into an increasingly antiquated model of the male as the primary earner, and the female as the primary caregiver. I was in my seventeenth year as a vice president at a national organization when I brought the kids home from Russia. Before that first year home ended, I resigned due to the unexpected emotional and physical demands of the kids. My husband worked long hours, carrying the pressure of provider.

The work/family/life balance is a common strain many couples experience once they have children. So is a loss of the way they were before becoming parents. I wonder if I looked like a stranger to my husband in my new role as a mother, whose business suits were collecting dust in the spare closet. Nurturing and managing the kids was endless. Asking for support and help became harder and harder to start doing while sinking in quicksand. "Have fun," he would often say as he left for work. I know he meant it, and would have liked the idea of us having a good time. I imagine he felt unappreciated for the work he was doing during the day, and never knew how much I needed and missed him. Eventually, I lost connection to him and the outside world, and our relationship couldn't integrate family life into "the way we were."

Marital strain can place an emotional burden on young children. For adoptees, this has added complexity as they come to the family with already vulnerable emotions in their disorganized world. Adoption brings challenges to a couple, like life assuredly can in other ways. What the marriage does depends on each individual and the couple unit, what they need, what is right for them, and what they actively choose with each new day, challenge, celebration, and endeavor.

A particular secret of marriage and adoption is that life is not necessarily different than that of other married couples with children. It can be sacred, fun, and extremely complicated. There are always three units to consider in a relationship: each individual partner and the couple unit. Stepping back and considering the health of your relationship with your partner is highly recommended before starting a family, including one that has the added complications of an adoptive one. This applies to you if you are single as well. If you are content as a single person or clear on what you want, you will have a more positive adoption experience. Neither of these options suggest your relationship status will go unchanged.

Intimacy in a relationship will need to transcend, (not replace) sex when you start a family. Mutual feelings of affection, commitment, and deep intimacy evolve passionate love into consummate love over time. It breeds a deeply satisfying contentment that has the strength to overcome cracks in the relationship where destructive characteristics, such as contempt, can enter. "Today, we turn to one person to provide what an entire village once did: a sense of grounding, meaning, and continuity. At the same time, we expect our committed relationships to be romantic as well as emotionally and sexually fulfilling. Is it any wonder that so many relationships crumble under the weight of it all," asked by relationship author, Esther Perel. True communication with your partner, the kind that takes effort and vulnerability, maintaining self awareness, and knowing how to get resourced will help sustain a vital, erotic and interdependent relationship. Individuals who are better adjusted in their marriages or relationships find co-parenting to be a more positive experience, thus promoting increased co-parenting integrity and decreased conflict.

WHILE YOU'RE WAITING...

How satisfied are you in the love category of your life, (whether you or involved with another or not)?

An adult's attachment style, formed in childhood through the attunement or mis-attunement with their parent, influences our adult relationship with others. It's especially valuable in how we show up in love relationships, and co-parenting. The awareness of your desires and needs being met is a treasure for your potentially adopted children, lover/spouse and yourself, whether you are married, coupled, single, or seeking. We are genetically programmed with a need to share life with someone. Psychiatrist and neuroscientist, Amir Levine, MD, describes the attachment styles in his book, *Attached*.

Anxious: People with an anxious attachment style have great capacity for emotional intimacy and get attached strongly and quickly.

Secure: Secure people are the most calm and confident of them all. They are comfortable with intimacy without being overly worried or jealous. They communicate effectively and they tend to keep an even keel without any major swings of moods or emotions.

Avoidant: Avoidants are torn between the willingnessfor closeness and the rejection of it. They also have a strong need for keeping their own space on top, which makes for uncomfortable intimacy in the relationship. Avoidants often put independence and autonomy before their intimate relationships.

Visit Dr. Levine's and Dr. Heller's website to take compatibility quize by deciphering your own and your partner's attachment style: https://www.attachedthe-book.com/wordpress/compatibility-quiz/

CHAPTER 10

RUPTURE AND REPAIR

After two plane rides, three hotels, five thousand miles, and over twenty hours of travel, Alex finally fell hard to sleep in the back of the car on the way to the house. We arrived late evening, and carried him to his new bed to sleep for twelve hours. Meanwhile, Daria sat on the couch, hyper-vigilant, broad-eyed watching everything. My mother in law had brought groceries over that evening, and continued to be of tremendous support to me during those first challenging years. Her background in child development was evidenced by how effectively she related to the kids, and their immediate comfort with her. She spent many afternoons with the kids, giving them her undivided attention, inquiry, and laughter. That relieved me to take care of things, but the moral support I got from her remains with me today. She conveyed her belief in me many times over, giving me hope about the future.

OUR HISTORY, OURSELVES

My mom was too ill to fully participate in the homecoming or caregiving of the children. I began caring for my mom at a very young age, while my older brother and sister, (kids themselves), took care of me as our parents were no longer together. My brother saved me from drowning when I crawled into the pool as a baby. Understanding that as a trauma combined with my mother's compromised state undoubtedly impacted my perception of her ability to care for me (and herself).

I recall experiencing deep sorrow when my sister, and then brother left for college. When he joined the army and went abroad, I was distraught. I've grown to appreciate and realize the way in which the two of them served as caregivers in my life. As they left home, I felt a sense of abandonment and helplessness in the responsibility of caring for my mother. My family was tethered together by concern for her health, and the desire for her love. The reactions and responses to her illness united us out of good intentions, but the fatigue of this schema on the family eventually created a temporary distance amongst family members.

"Wanting so ardently to make things right for her mother was, of course, that same mother's doing. Anna had so drawn Lily into her maternity, into her female ness and her magic, that Lily could not be faulted for wanting to fix everything, even if she didn't understand what was that needed fixing."
– Susannah Moore, *My Old Sweetheart*

This story further affirms the case for a parent to have a healthy relationship within oneself. A parent is a connection to life, the perceived singular source of survival for a child. When a child senses instability, they may subconsciously try to preserve their safety by taking care of their parent, for if the parent is okay, then the child perceives themselves as okay.

Unresolved, the role of rescuer and caretaker can establish an unhealthy blueprint for later adult relationships. A distressed state of preparedness for disaster is created, and one's inner identity and value becomes self-measured by taking care of others. The ability to reflect on the cycles of circular causality in a family system replaces blame with understanding, and ultimately, healing. If left unaddressed a compromised parent brings forth the stories and pains of their past into their relationship with their child. Limiting beliefs, such as being unworthy of love, fear of not being enough or too much, and fear of not being supported arise from unresolved core wounds, and slowly contaminate interpersonal relationships and other primary areas of one's life.

Understanding yourself, to the extent you can, before bringing children home and into the world is an indirect form of parenting well for your child. A mother under her own personal distress or unresolved pain who is parenting behavioral challenges of a hurt child will eventually debunk the "myth of maternal bliss," described by Anne Lamott, in which mothers are saints, martyrs and expectedly without flaw. The dark part of parenthood no one wants to talk about is the escalating frustration that can convert to yelling, grabbing a child by the arm, or slamming doors after repeated aggravations played out by an innocent toddler. In Daniel Goleman's book, "Emotional Intelligence," he cites the work of Dolf Zillmann referring to the "sequence of provocations." A parent can get to the end of their proverbial rope, after repeated minor incidences of behavioral challenges. Maintaining the priority of noticing and tending to the toll of stress, before it gets to this point, will help prevent the risk of parental rage.

As an adult, you can reconcile unresolved past wounds, and therefore, more fully empathize with and recognize an adoptive children's ingrained fear manifested in actions. Distinguished from being afraid, fear is subcutaneous, deeply rooted, and largely informed by the past, yet is about the future. Mark Nepo encourages the acceptance that "we are here to come apart and be put back together repeatedly." We were close to divinity at the beginning of life. Somehow, along the way, we fall via mistakes, betrayals or wounds; our wholeness - separates. In these states, one can feel alone, broken, not enough, or unlovable. Adoptive motherhood can add to the isolation in some scenarios.

Excessive or extreme separation is fertile soil for pain. This kind of suffering can lead to a seeking of more love, acceptance, accomplishments, things, food – anything we can control. Each of these acts are a distorted attempt to reconnect, living life, but not fully. Some say life is a search back to wholeness.

> *"Those who see all beings in themselves,*
> *And themselves in all beings,*
> *Relinquish hatred.*
> *How can the seeming diversity of life*
> *Delude the one who has seen its unity?"*
> **– Isha Upanishad 6-7**

WHILE YOU'RE WAITING...

In what ways are you carrying pain or resentment because of something that has occurred in the past?

The suggestion here is to lean into the rupture when you are ready. Get support if needed. Proceed with competence in traversing the full emotional range of discomfort, for the repair through reflection will allow for a broader capacity to parent a hurt child with compassion and lovingkindness.

Sadness can be messy, and felt deep in your bones. Sadness slows us down, and perhaps that is serendipitous. Sadness will be written into our narratives at some point in life. The experience of going within is about surrender to an unconstricted identity of oneself. Pretending to be okay when pain is underneath you can eventually make one unrecognizable to self and others. Understand sadness as a potential precursor to joy and acceptance. To know joy, we must know sadness; to be light, we must know our shadow. Kahil Gibran once said, "When you are sorrowful, look again in your heart, and you shall see that in truth you are weeping for that which has been your delight."

The two priorities in Zen Meditation are consistently sitting to quiet the mind and heart to consistently "sweep the garden." This means establishing and maintaining a state of "care" within, and then out to others. The *While You're Waiting* process is all about sweeping the inner garden. Jack Kornfield teaches forgiveness as a necessary element in cultivating a state of care for self and others that is helpful in noticing inner feelings and thoughts that may need healing in one's life. The following is adapted from the Forgiveness Meditation by Jack Kornfield.

FORGIVENESS OF OTHERS

There are many ways that I have hurt and harmed others, have betrayed or abandoned them, caused them suffering, knowingly or unknowingly, out of my pain, fear, anger, and confusion. See and feel the pain you have caused out of your own fear and confusion. Feel your own sorrow and regret. And then to each person in your mind repeat: I ask for your forgiveness, I ask for your forgiveness.

FORGIVENESS FOR YOURSELF

There are many ways that I have betrayed or abandoned myself many times through thought, word, or deed, knowingly or unknowingly. Feel the sorrow you have carried from this and sense that you can release these burdens. Extend forgiveness for each of them, one by one. Repeat to yourself: For the ways I have hurt myself through action or inaction, out of fear, pain and confusion, I now extend a full and heartfelt forgiveness. I forgive myself.

FORGIVENESS FOR THOSE WHO HAVE HURT OR HARMED YOU

There are many ways that I have been harmed by others, abused or abandoned, knowingly or unknowingly, in thought, word or deed. Let yourself picture and remember these many ways. Feel the sorrow you have carried from this past and sense that you can release this burden of pain by extending forgiveness when your heart is ready. Now say to yourself: I have carried this pain in my heart too long. To the extent that I am ready, I offer them forgiveness. To those who have caused me harm, I offer my forgiveness, I forgive you.

For some great pains you may not feel a release but only the burden and the anguish or anger you have held. Touch this softly. Be forgiving of yourself for not being ready to let go and move on. Forgiveness cannot be forced; it cannot be artificial. In time you can make the forgiveness meditation a regular part of your life, letting go of the past and opening your heart to each new moment with a wise *lovingkindness*.

CHAPTER 11

RESOLVE TO REVOLVE

The kids had only met me the summer before, and we spoke different languages. Their knowledge of me was the person removing them from the only home they knew. I believe that served as an inner conflict within the kids for a while, the juxtaposition of wanting to love their new mom, who was also the person that took them from their safe place. I found myself in a similar contrasting position, on the wildest ride I will ever have in shepherding the children into the rest of their lives. At the same time, it was the beginning of feeling alone amidst this expanded new role and world I was entering.

I have since realized the importance of developing a family narrative about how extended families came together, how we have persevered, what we were like as children, and other stories about our pasts can be healing and tether us together in a profound way. Dr. Duke, psychologist at Emory University, and his colleague, Dr. Fivush, conducted an extensive study on sharing family stories. Their overwhelming conclusion is "the more children knew about their family's history, the stronger their sense of control over their lives, the higher their self-esteem and the more successfully they believed their families functioned."

You will offer your truth, balanced with a responsibility in protecting the child's heart. This simply means exploring the narrative as it organically surfaces in place of forcing it. An attuned parent can effectively scaffold their child's discourse. Story telling is not something that comes naturally to all, but you must know yours intimately in order for it to continue to unfold with and nurture the adoption. For inspiration: visit www.storycorps.com, where family stories are recorded and archived; and their intergenerational movement: *The Great Thanksgiving Listen* inspiring children to record their elder's stories, which are preserved in The Library of Congress.

We began this process with a focus on your motivations for considering adoption and starting/expanding your family. Surely there have been many factors that have influenced your decision. On the other hand, maybe there is a significant part of the story that is continually left unsaid. As you reflect upon how your past has brought you here, we must also look at the future. It is exciting, and at the same time, it is understandable for you to have hopes and fears about the path ahead.

Exploring thoughts or concerns you may have, such as wanting a "baby of your own," or one that looks like you, diffuse the energy around it. Recognizing stigma that may surface in your experience with an adopted child lets you know if you are up for that challenge, or if you have other battles to tackle right now. You now know how to employ a self-agency for what matters to you. Your family-of-origin relationships can shape your current interpersonal ones and the parent-child relationship. The introduction to trauma and attachment may have surfaced some of your core wounds.

You now realize the importance in getting resourced to repair those inner ruptures, or become actively aware of them, so you are prepared to face those that may surface with an adoptive child.

You've also explored how you handle stress and the unexpected in life. Considering the complexity of defense strategies, which was introduced in Chapter Four, higher functioning defense responses, such as postponing or repressing attention to a conflict, may result in a temporarily satisfactory outcome. However, a less mature defense, such as a parent attributing characteristics he or she finds unacceptable in themselves onto their child can be psychologically taxing for both of them. The full range of defenses was not covered since this is not a clinical book on personality theory, yet recognizing the mature and less mature ways in which you or your child may employ a defense or coping skill is quite helpful.

Translating that into action, by shifting some of that stress, being open and asking for help is the challenge. You have hopefully come away with a more thorough understanding of the many components of your life that make you who you are today. There can be some peace found within self-inquiry and it can sur-face unrest. Recognizing to what degree your personal/emotional life is satisfactory and stable enough to begin the adoption process - will pay dividends in your life quality moving forward.

Oftentimes, it takes one too many falls or hiding for too long before we are willing to consider another angle from which to see ourselves. Unresolved inner unrest is psychologically expensive. With a contemplative prac-tice, you recognize your defenses, and you understand how to leverage your emotional intelligence and intu-ition. The benefit of an ongoing inventory will keep you close to self-love, an inner calmness, stability, and secu-rity within oneself, and therefore the ability to provide it for a child. The challenge moving forward is not shut-ting the door on the contemplative practice when things feel sticky, difficult, or complete. Cultivating an ongoing relationship with your innermost feelings and intention-ality has a way of richly painting all experiences.

Although, this book does not attempt to serve as an adoption manual, it is entirely important to introduce the concept of trauma and its effect on the developing brain of a child. You learned about how a child from hurt can project their own fears through behaviors of acting out, and shutting down. You learned that you cannot replace the first day of their life, and any beyond when they were without a parent. However, through a strong relationship with yourself and your child, the trajectory can be wonderfully positive. Having children can set you on a path of driving through life like a machine rather than a human being. You will need support, and must ask for it. Forcing yourself to slow down and become grounded sounds simple. You will need the patience of a farmer and the ability to visualize yourself and your child as kind and both anchored in love.

WHILE YOU'RE WAITING...

Are you ready to move forward with adoption and surrender the attachment to the outcome of your decision?

The decision to adopt is informed by your past, layered with compassion, inspired by sweet optimism, and driven by your fierce self-determinism. The ability to return to your center, again and again, will give you the comfort and confidence in your ability to discern well. The exploration you've had into the emotional categories has helped you become more reflective of the experiences that you may struggle to work with as a parent. You have new insight into your blind spots and know to pay care-full attention as they arise. As you continue, the next steps will be to consider:

- What are your fears about adoption?
- How has your view of adoption has changed from the beginning of this book?
- Which areas of your life do you need to pay special attention to moving forward?
- What are your hopes for the next step in your adoption?
- Can you experience being present with your emotions, needs, and truth in place of anticipation and rumination?
- What primary element of your self and life are you most satisfied with in this moment?

CHAPTER 12

THE POSTSCRIPT

*F**ree from needing to know all the steps or where they may lead, she took one...*

Dear Beautiful Dove,

You arrived here out of your hunger for adoption advice, only to realize this book is more about you, your heart and your mind in the midst of an enormous life event. You learned about various aspects of adoption in this book while you agreed to look within yourself, notice your responses, and listen to your emotions. Learning how to pause and deeply listen to your own mind is one of the first and most critical things you can do in an act of self-love, and therefore the ability to love another.

Hopefully, you have learned about the importance of your self-agency, have experienced a remembrance of wholeness, and developed a contemplative practice that you can sustain further - independently and with support. The process is unending. My wish for you is that you have a loving relationship with yourself to traverse the unknown of the future, the judgement of others, the pain and joy of your child, and asking for what you need in the dream and adventure of becoming a vibrant and loving parent.

Turns out the bliss found in ignorance is momentary. Your willingness to take the time to look within, listen, and contemplate your narrative in what brings you to the adoption process may have surfaced some old wounds, more fear about the adoption, more excitement about the adoption, more confusion, more clarity or a mixture therein. I hope it strengthens your hope. The benefit of turning inward and getting exceptionally friendly with your inner world is higher-level living, but it's not always easy to sustain. Taking action, doing not thinking, can feel more concrete and productive. There is a time for that. Clarity comes via relative ease in moving through the questions, but it also arrives when the spontaneous inquiry surfaces.

I realize the steps and questions I asked of you cannot all be addressed in the period between now and when you bring your child home. Remember, life breaks us open again and again. The opportunity in returning to the invitation of refining the relationship with yourself will surface again and again. Just when you think you've hit your stride as a mom, you get knocked to your knees, just when you think your child is thriving, they lash out at you because you are the safest place for them to unload their anger, hurt and confusion.

I love the phrase, "innocence is lost, but not forgotten." It took awhile for wisdom to fully integrate with the naivety that informed my early life. The combination of innocence and wisdom now breeds hopefulness and ability. A remembrance of wholeness does not mean something is broken. Self-evolution arises from repetitive acts of intention, discovering mastery in the mundane, and joy in the ordinary. I recognize how hard it is to interrupt the beautiful dream of adopting and having a child. Think of this as a tune-up and tank filling for a beautiful and adventurous road trip. The benefit is living a life rich with authenticity and a genuine love for self, and therefore others.

Thank you so very much for choosing to adopt a child. While you're waiting… so is the child. My inspiration for writing this book is plentiful, and one of the reasons is that I believe there are so many compassionate people available to provide love and care for orphaned children. Equally, I want the children to have the healthiest and strongest chance at a rich life. Cultivating parental attunement and emotional health is a prerequisite for the life role as an adoptive parent. This requires us to do the inner work to become guardians of our children's hearts. Realize you are matter-full, and join me in the ongoing work at becoming masterful in listening within and with others.

Beautiful soul, you are the Dove, representing peace, fidelity and love. Seeing two or more doves symbolizes the powerful wisdom found within their representation. Offered below is a beautiful letter written by an unknown author, who is believed to be an adoptive mother. It unites us all like a flight of doves, a right of passage into the compassion and community of adoptive and birth moms everywhere. Welcome, I'm so very honored to be a part of your journey.

Once there were two women
Who never knew each other.
One you do not remember,
The other you call mother.
Two different lives
Shaped to make yours one.
One became your guiding star,
The other became your sun.
The first gave you life
And the second taught you to live it.
The first gave you a need for love
And the second was there to give it.
One gave you a nationality,
The other gave you a name.
One gave you a seed of talent,
The other gave you an aim.
One gave you emotions,
The other calmed your fears.
One saw your first sweet smile,
The other dried your tears.
One gave you up -
It was all that she could do.

The other prayed for a child
And God led her straight to you.
And now you ask me
Through your tears,
The age-old question
Through the years:
Heredity or environment
Which are you the product of?
Neither, my darling - neither,
Just two different kinds of love.

Big Love,
Me

ACKNOWLEDGMENTS

Deep gratitude to my beloved friends and family for how we listen to and share our stories with one another. Especially Susie for coming to help that first week and beyond, and for your devotion to our beautiful friendship. Your adopted son hit the jackpot with winning your resilience and unconditional love. And, Crista traveling miles and miles for the years it is taking us to figure everything out about life, Erika who has the ability to convert tears to laughter in one flip of her unicorn wand, Laura for knowing me inside out and being a role model in life and motherhood, Melody for your unwavering loyalty and love, wholehearted wisdom, and always offering to "drop everything" to come together; our work in the world is not finished.

Thank you Anna, Jack, Janis, Fenton and Linda for spending quality time with the kids. The way you love and positively regard the kids helped crystalize the secure feeling of being held by family. Thank you Johnny for taking such good care of me and saving my life. Thank you dad for your humility, kindness, and being the founding and singular member of my fan club. Thank you mom, the constant affection you gave me has paid dividends in my life over and over again by preserving gentleness - even in the shadows of life.

Thank you Judy for the decades of hugs you have provided to orphans in Russia, and for an unexpected sweet space to land at The Learning Tree. From the wells of my heart, thank you to all the teachers, healers, coaches, classmates, other school parents who embraced, taught, helped and included our children, particularly as they navigated the foreign environment they were thrust into at such a young age. Thank you for those who sustained compassion amongst what couldn't be understood. You all have saved the day many times.

Thank you Hope International for uniting our family. Thank you to the people in my life that believed our unique experience could be helpful to others and encouraged me to write this book. Thank you to Angela, and my editor, Cory, for helping me bring this book to print. Thank you Marc for staying in the shadows with me. And to SB, for keeping the path lit, calling all the angels down to earth, and loving like the moon.

THANK YOU

Thank you for exploring the topic of adoption whether you are a expectant parent, a parent, or have general or professional interest. Our story is unique to us with the characteristics of sibling group adoption, non-infant child adoption, and international adoption. Your experience will be beautifully different.

I've received questions about how the children are doing now. As of the completion of this book, they are truly thriving in high school with friends, sports and grades. They are funny and do the same things that other teenagers do: the things we expect and the things we don't understand! Life is beautifully imperfect, traces of our adoption dynamic are present, and we still make mistakes. I am figuring this "chapter" out for now. I am beyond grateful, and highly optimistic. I often want to make them a shirt that reads, "Wish they could see me now!"

I'd love to hear your story. Please visit our private forum for those deciding, waiting and coming home at https://www.facebook.com/groups/theadoptionoption/.

Sign up for articles and adoption information from Viv at www.whileyourewaitingbook.com. Please contact Viv via the website for agency and group consultations and speaking engagements.

About the Author

Viv is a psychotherapist with more than a decade of experience in mind body health. She studied counseling psychology at The Family Institute of Northwestern University and is currently pursuing her doctorate in clinical psychology.

Experienced in treating individuals struggling with trauma, relationship issues, and life transitions, she draws from her research and training in psychodynamic theory, attachment theory, and interpersonal neurobiology to work collaboratively with her patients.

Viv lives in Dallas, Texas, with her two children who keep her current on memes, rock-n-roll, basketball, and the reminder to always listen gently.

*Given the private nature of the author's psychotherapy work, Viv is used as the author's pseudonym.

ABOUT DIFFERENCE PRESS

Difference Press is the exclusive publishing arm of The Author Incubator, an educational company for entrepreneurs – including life coaches, healers, consultants, and community leaders – looking for a comprehensive solution to get their books written, published, and promoted. Its founder, Dr. Angela Lauria, has been bringing to life the literary ventures of hundreds of authors-in-transformation since 1994.

A boutique-style self-publishing service for clients of The Author Incubator, Difference Press boasts a fair and easy-to-understand profit structure, low-priced author copies, and author-friendly contract terms. Most importantly, all of our #incubatedauthors maintain ownership of their copyright at all times.

LET'S START A MOVEMENT WITH YOUR MESSAGE

In a market where hundreds of thousands of books are published every year and are never heard from again, The Author Incubator is different. Not only do all Difference Press books reach Amazon bestseller status, but all of our authors are actively changing lives and making a difference.

Since launching in 2013, we've served over 500 authors who came to us with an idea for a book and were able to write it and get it self-published in less than 6 months. In addition, more than 100 of those books were picked up by traditional publishers and are now available in book stores. We do this by selecting the highest quality and highest potential applicants for our future programs.

Our program doesn't only teach you how to write a book – our team of coaches, developmental editors, copy editors, art directors, and marketing experts incubate you from having a book idea to being a published, bestselling author, ensuring that the book you create can actually make a difference in the world. Then we give you the training you need to use your book to make the difference in the world, or to create a business out of serving your readers.

ARE YOU READY TO MAKE A DIFFERENCE?

You've seen other people make a difference with a book. Now it's your turn. If you are ready to stop watching and start taking massive action, go to http://theauthorincubator.com/apply/.

"Yes, I'm ready!"

DIFFERENCE
P R E S S

OTHER BOOKS BY
DIFFERENCE PRESS

Going Home: Saying Goodbye with Grace and Joy When You Know Your Time is Short by Michael G. Giovanni, Jr.

Get Happier, Fitter, and off the Meds Now!: 7-Steps to Improved Health and a Body You Love by Ell Graniel

Healed: A Divinely Inspired Path to Overcoming Cancer by Pamela Herzer, M.A.

Live Healthy With Hashimoto's Disease: The Natural Ayurvedic Approach to Managing Your Autoimmune Disorder by Vikki Hibberd

I Left My Toxic Relationship – Now What?: The Step-By-Step Guide to Starting over and Living on Your Own by Heather J. Kent

Sign Your First Coaching Client: Steps to Launch Your New Career by Carine Kindinger

Find Your Beloved: Your Guide to Attract True Love by Rosine Kushnick

My Toddler Has Stopped Having so Many Tantrums: The Mother's Guide to Finding Joy in Parenting by Susan Jungermann

In the Eye of a Relationship Storm: Know What to Do in an Abusive Situation by Jackquline Ann

My Clothes Fit Again!: The Overworked Women's Guide to Losing Weight by Sue Seal

How Do I Survive?: 7 Steps to Living After Child Loss by Patricia Sheveland

Your Life Matters: Learn to Write Your Memoir in 8 Easy Steps by Junie Swadron

Medication Detox: How to Live Your Best Health, Simplified by Rachel Reinhart Taylor, M.D.

Keeping Well: An Anti-Cancer Guide to Remain in Remission by Brittany Wisniewski